Pierre-Auguste Renoir

Alix Wood

WINDMILL
BOOKS

New York

Published in 2016 by **Windmill Books**, An Imprint of Rosen Publishing
29 East 21st Street, New York, NY 10010

Editor for Alix Wood Books: Eloise Macgregor
Designer: Alix Wood

Photo Credits: Cover, 1 © public domain; 4 top, 5, 12, 25 © Musée
d'Orsay; 4 bottom © PetitPoulailler; 6 © Wadsworth Atheneum; 7 top,
10 © Metropolitan Museum of Art; 7 bottom © National Museum,
Stockholm; 9 © Alte Nationalgalerie, Berlin; 11 © Courtauld Institute; 13
© Gorrk; 14-15 © The Phillips Collection; 16 © Dollar Photo Club; 17 ©
Art Institute of Chicago; 19 © The National Gallery; 21, 22 © Museum
of Fine Arts, Boston; 23 © nga/Mr. and Mrs. Paul Mellon;
26 © Bequest of Charlotte Gina Abrams; 27 top © The Barnes
Foundation, Philadelphia; 29 top © nga/Ailsa Mellon Bruce Collection;
29 bottom © Bibliothèque Nationale de France; all other images are in
the public domain

Cataloging-in-Publication Data

Wood, Alix.
Pierre-Auguste Renoir / by Alix Wood.
p. cm. — (Artists through the ages)
Includes index.
ISBN 978-1-4777-5599-0 (pbk.)
ISBN 978-1-4777-5598-3 (6 pack)
ISBN 978-1-4777-5522-8 (library binding)
1. Renoir, Auguste, — 1841-1919 — Juvenile literature.
2. Painters — France — Biography — Juvenile literature.
I. Wood, Alix. II. Title.
ND553.R45 W66 2016
759.4—d23

Manufactured in the United States of America
CPSIA Compliance Information: Batch #WS15WM:
For Further Information contact Windmill Books, New York, New York at 1-866-478-0556

Contents

Who Was Renoir?

Pierre-Auguste Renoir was born in Limoges, France, in 1841. His father was a **tailor** and his mother was a **seamstress**. He was the couple's sixth child, but two older siblings died as infants. His family moved to Paris when he was still young.

Self-portrait, 1876

Map of the World

North America

Europe

Asia

Africa

South America

Australia

Paris

Limoges

FRANCE

Limoges is famous for its beautiful painted porcelain.

In Paris, Renoir's house was near the famous art museum, the Louvre. He often visited the museum. At school, Renoir was a talented artist. His parents found him an **apprenticeship** at a porcelain painter's at age 13. He studied drawing in his free time. He learned to decorate plates with bouquets of flowers. Later he worked painting fans and cloth panels for **missionaries** to hang in churches.

Artist Friends

Renoir had saved a little money. At age 19, he started evening classes at the École des Beaux-Arts, a famous art school. He also took painting lessons from Charles Gleyre. At Gleyre's studio, Renoir made friends with three other young artists, Frédéric Bazille, Claude Monet, and Alfred Sisley.

Frédéric Bazille Painting at his Easel, 1867

Good Friends

Renoir and his three painter friends often met up with artists Camille Pissarro and Paul Cézanne. They all had similar ideas about art. They shared **studios**, shared ideas, and gave each other encouragement.

The artist friends liked to paint outdoors. Most traditional artists painted in their studios. New techniques meant paint could now be bought in tubes rather than having to be mixed from powders. This made painting outdoors easier.

The friends often painted each other. Renoir did this portrait of his friend, *Claude Monet Painting in His Garden at Argenteuil*, 1873.

Painting Trips Together

La Grenouillère, 1869

Monet created this **sketch** of an almost identical view to Renoir's painting below. The two friends must have been working side by side.

La Grenouillère, 1869. Renoir's painting of a popular floating café in Paris.

Renoir's Early Style

Renoir's paintings are full of light and color. Renoir was an **Impressionist**. Impressionists often painted using bold brushstrokes of color. The background of the painting opposite is typical of an Impressionist style. He did not feel the need to paint the detail of each leaf.

In 1867, Renoir met Lise Tréhot, a seamstress who became his model. He did many paintings of her, including *The **Bohemian***, opposite. Renoir, himself, was considered a Bohemian. A Bohemian is a person who is interested in art, music, and books, and who likes an informal life, ignoring the usually accepted ways of behaving.

Wartime

In 1870, France's war with Germany meant Renoir had to take a break from his work. He was **drafted** into the cavalry but he soon fell ill. Renoir never had to fight, unlike his friend Bazille, who was killed that November.

The Bohemian, 1868

The Impressionists

After the war ended, Renoir went back to Paris and his art. The leading Paris art exhibition, the Salon, did not like the friends' work and would not exhibit any. In 1874, they decided to set up their own exhibition. An art **critic** reviewed their show and said the works were "impressions" rather than finished paintings. He meant it as an insult, but the name "Impressionists" stuck.

Meeting the Right People

Madame Charpentier and Her Children, 1878

The exhibition was not a success, but Renoir met some wealthy supporters. Publisher Georges Charpentier and his wife invited him to parties where he found **portrait commissions** from the couple's friends.

The Theater Box, 1874

Painting Paris Life

Renoir liked to paint people enjoying themselves. The Moulin de la Galette was in Montmartre, an area that was then just outside Paris. There was a windmill on top of the hill and a good view of Paris below. People would meet there and dance. "Moulin" means "windmill" in French.

Dance at the Moulin de la Galette, 1876

Renoir captured the joyful atmosphere at the dance. His lively, bright brushstrokes make the scene come alive. He put many of his friends in the painting. Renoir painted at least the first sketch on the spot. A friend once said that the wind on the hill constantly threatened to blow the canvas away!

Renoir's painting was shown at the Impressionist exhibition in 1877. The blurred painting didn't impress the art critics. The work has since been called one of the masterpieces of Impressionism.

Money Trouble

During the period when Renoir was producing some of his best work, he had money problems. Renoir once wrote to his friend Bazille saying of himself and Monet, "Although we don't eat every day, I am still quite cheerful."

A galette is a type of bread from the area around the Moulin de la Galette. It was an inexpensive lunch for Renoir and his artist friends.

Success

By the end of the 1870s, Renoir had become a fashionable painter. His painting *Madame Charpentier and Her Children* was accepted by the Salon in 1879.

Renoir's *Luncheon of the Boating Party* was included in the Seventh Impressionist Exhibition in 1882, and was identified as the best painting in the show by three critics.

Renoir again painted his friends into the picture. Aline Charigot (pictured playing with a small dog) later became his wife.

Luncheon of the Boating Party, 1880-1881

Colors and Shadows

It is thought that Renoir only used five colors in his **palette**. His work as a porcelain painter taught him how to mix his colors well. Impressionists used light colors. They did not like to use black. Renoir once said of he and his fellow Impressionists: "One morning one of us had run out of black; and that was the birth of Impressionism."

Shadows

Renoir and Monet realized that shadows were not black or brown. They were made up of the colors of objects around them. Critics at the time were appalled at the colors they used for shadows!

Can you see any black in the painting opposite? What colors has Renoir used to create shadows and dark areas?

Two Sisters, 1881, was originally called *On the Terrace*. The two girls are not actually sisters. The painting was named *Two Sisters* by Paul Durand-Ruel, who bought the work.

A Change of Style

As Renoir began to make money from his commissions, he spent some time traveling. He went to Algeria, Spain, Italy, and the south of France. He visited art galleries and studied work by great artists such as Raphael. The paintings he saw inspired him to try a change of style.

Renoir decided his Impressionist style could not show the satin look of skin. Renoir's new style is often called his "Ingres" period as it resembles work by Jean-Auguste-Dominique Ingres. His new style was smooth, with no obvious brushstrokes, like in the painting opposite. Which style do you prefer?

The Umbrellas

Renoir began this painting in 1880 using his old style. He then altered the painting in around 1885. X-ray images of the painting show he added the umbrellas, and changed the woman on the left's dress to remove some lace and make it plainer.

The Umbrellas, 1885-6

Dance at Bougival

Renoir continued to paint using his new style, but in *Dance at Bougival* he used the bright colors of his Impressionist style. *Dance at Bougival* is nearly 6 feet (1.8 m) tall! The painting was one of a set of three commissioned by art dealer Paul Durand-Ruel. The others were called *Dance in the City* and *Dance in the Country.*

Model Artist

Renoir painted artists' model Suzanne Valadon in several of his paintings. She is the woman dancing in *Dance at Bougival.* She also modeled for his friends. Valadon studied their techniques and eventually became one of the leading painters of the day.

Still Life with Basket of Apples, Vase of Flowers and Grapes, 1928, by Valadon

Dance at
Bougival, 1883

Painting Flowers

Renoir was an expert flower painter. His first paintings were the flowers that he painted on porcelain when he was a young apprentice. He once told a critic, "I just let my mind rest when I paint flowers."

Last Word

It is said that Renoir's last word was "flowers," when an assistant brought a bouquet of roses from his garden and put them on his bedroom windowsill.

Mixed Flowers in an Earthenware Pot, 1869

Flowers in a Vase, 1866

A Family Man

As Renoir's fame grew, he began to settle down. He married his longtime girlfriend, Aline Charigot, in 1890, when he was almost 50 years old. The couple lived in Montmartre and raised their five-year-old son, Pierre, there. They went on to have two more sons, Claude and Jean.

In the early 1890s, admirers of Renoir's work became angry that the French State had never purchased any of his art. In 1892, his supporters organized a commission from the state, and *Girls at the Piano*, opposite, was bought and placed in the Musée du Luxembourg.

Layers

After 1890, Renoir changed his style again. He began to paint using thin layers of color. This made the outlines appear to dissolve into his backgrounds. *Girls at the Piano* was painted during this period.

Girls at the Piano, 1892. Renoir painted three other versions of this painting, and two sketches. Known by the artist as "repetitions," they were done to sell to dealers and collectors.

Later Years

As he got older Renoir developed rheumatoid arthritis. This causes pain, swelling, and stiffness in the joints. Renoir found it hard to paint. Eventually his hands were unable to pick up a paintbrush. He hired an assistant to place a brush in his hands. He never stopped painting. Renoir bought a house in Cagnes, southern France, where the warm weather was better for his health.

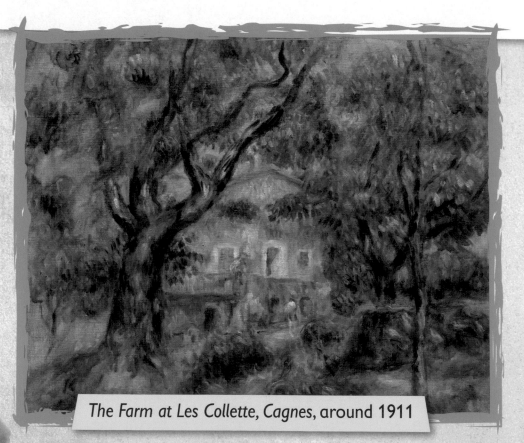

The Farm at Les Collette, Cagnes, around 1911

His Children

Renoir's growing family gave him inspiration. This painting shows his sons Pierre (standing), and Jean (in white) with their mother, nanny Gabrielle Renard, and a friend (in red). It was the fashion to dress young boys in girls' clothes at the time!

The Artist's Family, 1896

Jean Renoir, 1901

Renoir painted this portrait of seven-year-old son Jean when he was out of school with a cold. To keep him occupied, he gave him a pencil and paper so he could draw some animals.

Renoir's Legacy

Renoir illness became worse and he spent his last years in a wheelchair. He also developed problems with his eyesight. He died in Cagnes in 1919, at age 78. Shortly before his death he visited the Louvre in Paris. He saw his paintings hanging there, among the great artists. It must have been a proud moment.

Family Fame

His children became very successful. Jean became a filmmaker, Pierre became an actor, and Claude became a ceramic artist. Pierre's son Claude also became a well-known filmmaker.

Renoir produced several thousand paintings over his lifetime, including some of the most popular works in the history of art. He is one of the most important painters who belonged to his Impressionist group of friends.

Pierre-Auguste Renoir

Alix Wood

Peaches on a Plate, around 1904

By the end of his life Renoir had made a good living from his art, but his paintings sell for millions at auction now. Renoir continued to learn and perfect his art. At age 72 he said, "I am just learning how to paint!"

Glossary

apprenticeship
(uh-PREN-tis-ship)
A period in which a
young person works with
an experienced person to
learn a skill or trade.

Bohemian
(boh-HEE-mee-un)
A person (such as an
artist or writer) who
does not have a
typical lifestyle.

critic (KRIH-tik)
A person who writes
his or her opinion
about something.

drafted (DRAFT-ed)
The selection of people
for a special purpose, such
as joining the military.

Impressionist
(im-PREH-shuh-nist)
An artist who
concentrates on the
impression of a scene
using unmixed primary
colors and small
brushstrokes to
simulate light.

missionaries
(MIH-shuh-nayr-eez)
People sent to another
country to tell people
about a certain faith.

palette (PA-lit)
The selection of paints
that an artist chooses to
paint with.

portrait commissions
(POR-tret
kuh-MIH-shunz)
Being asked to paint
a picture of a person,
usually for money.

seamstress
(SEEM-strus)
A woman who sews
for a living.

sketch (SKECH)
A quick drawing.

studios (STOO-dee-ohz)
The rooms or buildings
where an artist works.

tailor (TAY-lor)
A person whose
occupation is making
clothes or making
adjustments in clothes.

Websites

For web resources related to the
subject of this book, go to:
www.windmillbooks.com/weblinks
and select this book's title.

Read More

Boutan, Mila. *Renoir and Me*. London, UK: A&C Black, 2010.

Kelly, True. *Pierre-Auguste Renoir: Paintings That Smile* (Smart About Art). New York, NY: Grosset & Dunlap, 2005.

Wax, Wendy. *Renoir and the Boy with the Long Hair*. Hauppauge, NY: Barron's Educational Series, 2007.

Index